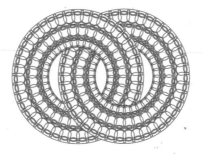

DEKE

DANGLE

DIVE

DEKE
DANGLE
DIVE

GIBSON
FAY-LEBLANC

CAVANKERRY
PRESS

CavanKerry Press Ltd.
Fort Lee, New Jersey
www.cavankerrypress.org

Publisher's Cataloging-In-Publication Data
(Prepared by The Donohue Group, Inc.)
Names: Fay-LeBlanc, Gibson, 1974- author.
Title: Deke dangle dive / Gibson Fay-LeBlanc.
Description: First edition. | Fort Lee, New Jersey : CavanKerry Press, 2021.
Identifiers: ISBN 9781933880853
Subjects: LCSH: Diseases—Poetry. | Fatherhood—Poetry. | Brotherliness—Poetry. | Masculinity—Poetry. | American poetry—21st century. | LCGFT: Poetry.
Classification: LCC PS3606.A953 D45 2021 | DDC 811/.6—dc23

Cover Photo © Daniel Wirgård/Stocksy United
Cover and interior text design by Ryan Scheife, Mayfly Design
First Edition 2021, Printed in the United States of America

CavanKerry Press is grateful for the support it receives from the New Jersey State Council on the Arts.

Also by Gibson Fay-LeBlanc

Death of a Ventriloquist (2012)

For my brother Leland Fay, 1970–2020

CONTENTS

1

2

3

4

5

1

deke, *n*.:
In Ice Hockey, deceptive movement or feint that induces an opponent to move out of position. Origin: 1960s: shortened form of decoy.

—Oxford English Dictionary

For poetry makes nothing happen: it survives
In the valley of its making where executives
Would never want to tamper, flows on south
From ranches of isolation and the busy griefs,
Raw towns that we believe and die in; it survives,
A way of happening, a mouth.

—W. H. Auden

Wing and a Prayer

Hook me up to a current I felt
once: birdsong so quiet it seemed
an echo of birdsong

or a creek made of air
the same temperature as a body—
a silent humming I walked through.

I'm supposed to let whatever
happens be what I want
but I still want, I want, I want

my brother's cells to stop their war
on each other. I want a poet
I missed too much when here.

I want the body of a woman
down the block to come back
so she can see her kids grow up

and they know they're seen. Deep
in my shallow root system
all of this is so far beyond

my small tangle of electric streets
where one raindrop pushed to one side
of one honey locust leaf can mean

somewhere someone dies of thirst
and somewhere else thunder becomes
a god again. I always want rest,

oh you godless godhead, positron,
annihilation, ether, or stream—
bottomless, unnamable—but I will

sit here as long as it takes and watch
for any drip, flutter, or tick
that could be your approving nod.

Hockey Poem

The goalie—sixties and fit, his graying mustache
leaping as he spoke—said, *No fucking talk*

about books here, to two defensemen
breaking down a novel. The room—we were

cinching shoulder pads, grabbing helmets—
roared. If you haven't been in this locker room,

here follows the list of subjects allowed: sex lives
with detail, deer or moose hunting, barrooms,

and hockey—kids, adult, professional, pond,
women's. *We're twenty-first century*

hockey players, I said, and then, *I read*
this wonderful poem the other day. We roared

again. I wasn't kidding but wanted the roar.
Dear Committees, keep your fucking medals

for reading poems or writing them—someday
I'll deke that goalie—catlike at six on a Thursday,

swiveling, kicking out puck after puck—
I'll crush a body, sprint the boards and swing

in front of him, show him the forehand
twitch and switch and slip puck into net

then I'll deliver lines on a man who finds
and kisses his brother, and the goalie's heart will leap

and flutter in the way he thought could never
happen outside this brutal, beautiful game.

Unwritten

In a poem I haven't written yet, my brother
convinces me to put on hockey equipment—
helmet to girdle to kneepads—and shoots
and shoots and shoots in the driveway, the puck

bouncing off me. In the poem I haven't written
for my brother, but plan to, we throw haymakers
on a hill; he headlocks me on grass; I whip
hardballs at his back; we scratch and gouge until

a boy jabs his finger at me, and my brother
swings at teeth too big for that kid's mouth.
In the poem I won't let myself write,
I say why I haven't written it, listing

to my left with a tonnage in the bulkhead
of bullshit that's shifted, before admitting
that I did, do, will, see him with a little
brother's eye, looking through isinglass.

In the poem that doesn't exist, I smile
rather than ask why one summer he slogged
at Gold Coast Dogs and walked the beach alone;
I number the cracked bricks in our apartments

and admit all nicknames he gave me, even
G-string. I wish for red foothills, more hours
we shared while our sons dueled with swords
and wands and bikes and leapt from leaning forts.

In the poem I don't write, and the one I'm left with
while the shadows of grander ones gesture on walls,
you're worried from sleep by phantom pain and real
pain and scads of pills and insurance papers,

and I get down on my knees and pray, Lee,
to all I barely believe, because how else
will there be decades ahead to be brothers
in this poem I don't write, then don't write more.

Making Nothing: So Much Depends

The red wheelbarrow now rust-bitten
won't make me reverberate

like wind peeling a silver maple,
or know what my son means to say

when he play-by-plays a baseball game,
or understand Joyce. It won't stitch

a friend's atrial hole or keep eyes
from a headless metal statue down the street.

I'll fill it with all the evidence,
but its chain-link rattle can enter lips, pass

tongue, teeth, back, back, up and down, fall
into dark rivers and all the lit, abandoned boulevards

that lead the way to an old drive-in
closed for all seasons—sky-sized

screen stretched across lodgepole spines—and drop us
in the middle of a movie—the dialogue

low, edges blurred—filmed in a color never
seen: fantastical, world-weary, bluer than blue.

Mock Heroic

I knew a girl who came
from a tower of a home

in Cartagena: trust fund,
no one had laid a hand

on her. All they did, all,
each night at bed, was tell

her to keep who she was
locked inside her seas

so no one would see it.
Granite terror of that

secret. Wild horse eyes
in the night. It's so easy

to make broken people.
I watch my boys mop all

the syrup with syrup
vehicles. How can I keep

them from fearing—no one
can make someone else know—

their own pale underparts,
their own ladderless hearts?

High Forest State Marginal

I fiddle a radio dial in answer
to a question no one asks how
why where what happened to bring
you lower than median grass and soot-
crusted snow the shiver your whole
body trembles with when a truck
muscles past which is also as long
as I see your face sign eyes
looking not looking looking not

High Forest State Marginal
some of us want a law in order
to not see you I would feel better
fail better too my boys backseat
like birds *what should we do what should*
we do nothing though one day I
talk big church charity program
something nothing the lines the lines
in your face the steel ingots the cracks

I repeat four street names like a chant
High Forest State Marginal
I tell a story in a car
needle spoon ink fist
it's all I know to do *bottle*
cot bottle needle the only way
to see not see you there is
nothing to us but wishes wind
cardboard cloth words their lack

Making Nothing: Bright Wings

At twenty-one there lived no
evidence that I should write, no
gift, no one asking me to give
the dearest deep down things

or myself permission to skip
a lab and admit that medical school
was someone else's dream I then now
did not need to have, hold, keep

except that I knew a girl; except
that college let me escape a family
in pieces, like almost every
plate, bowl, or dish I'd held;

except that I needed evidence
that I felt things, that I had
a life inside my life, and, and—
dear misspent youth, dear unshodded days—

I needed sound flicking in the tinder
and springing forth from tips
of grass and memories with teeth
and there was so much rain in Worcester

that I was bare, muddy, bent double
because I, I, from a long line of fakers
found a place I couldn't. I knew those
terrible words would lead me on, on.

Luck

1

Tonight my stick finds puck
after puck: some wobbling,

some slapped at, some fast
and low and caught in stride—

even two plucked from air:
gifts. Four in all feel

a net's rope arms, are made true.
No one in the stands to shout

2

Lucky Julius, which is what
my brother used to call me

after I drew an ace
or threw in a three off

the backboard or dribbled
a grounder into prickers,

the cheapest home run
ever. Today they shoot

lasers into his brain
and my shot pings the post

3

and goes in, of course.
I know the goal does not

matter: our guts push out
over girdles and after

we talk chiropractors
and knees. That Julius,

from *The Prince*, a pope,
moved armies with-

out thought or care, which is
one way to be lucky.

4

But how not to keep
score: two kids, a wife.

He just turned forty-two.
We puff, wince, and swear

on the bench. We try not to
wonder when thunder will surge

through limbs, and our long sticks
will forget hands, pucks, speed.

At Sea

for Lee

Keel, you were under me sunk deep
       so as not to tip or flip or let
salt water rush through the galley or
       angled berth in the bow.
Navigation keeps your now
       possible death in formless distance.
I can't hear, can't taste, can't smell what all
       hovers in the air—polished glass
holds it back as strings and horns
       fall from hidden speakers, jazz
asking me to close eyes, forget
       buffleheads on swells—and each
time I think the water may
       not rise, roll, and break, it does.
It does. Clouds combed into cornrows,
       held in place by a force I can't
see, can't conceive. My mind, my boat
       can't hold. How can I fathom a world
without you, ballast, brother, in it?

Fearful Symmetry

Today they track me—dull hungers:
these shoulders, these arts, all tigers:

the familiar eyes, a metal bed,
and a fresh scar across his head.

That one has the yellow razored
hair of a girl who's been humored

and ignored. One more a rippling flank
and serious paws, homeless, by the bank

on High. Don't read his sign. Make your
own apex predator. Give me a tour

of rubble and abandoned blocks,
bodies stacked in fields, clocks

that never once knew how to work.
I'll listen as well as any clerk

schooled in the art of hating what
registers in his dilating gut.

How to Deke

The craftiest players know—stutter
step, sudden speed, the body
plus boards a false clue—never
have the same pattern, but stay steady

enough inside the quick
—twitch, pivot, push, spring—
to hear a scratch before a stick's
poke check. Switchback, then swing

between the legs of that colossus,
scissor, swizzle, and fire the puck
so fast it rises to a mark
no one—not the goalie, not us—
expects, and you will light
(arms raised) our red red light.

2

Stay

Out past where human trails end
in snow-packed woods where light flicks
on and off between trunks in slim bands,

while my kids sit and sprint and sink
at school and my wife and lover
lays hands on the healthy and the sick,

I follow Our Lady of the Fur
in Infinite Directions, forget
who or what or why or where

and talk inside my head. I meet
my brother on the path, awl
in hand, poking holes in a casket;

I see two friends that grief makes small:
one's father dropped in mid-run,
the other's took three years to fall.

/ / /

Winter world without end, you've won
nothing. Your name addled, sullied—
frozen word even the trees shun.

/ / /

Later I fall into bed, potbellied,
ungodly, wordless, with velocity
and recall how all day a doilied

chambermaid brought sausages and brie
when two small boys with a bell called,
then I remember that maid was me,

mildly cross but still tending the salted
goldfish, cleaning orange crumbs,
making sure chocolate milk was served.

When the dark lifts, my hours numb,
my lover hauls her body up
like any other day, succumbs

to bodies ill and sick, a pileup
of screens and stacks of virtual paper
explaining who needs actual help.

                /   /   /

Field-guided world, ice-river whistler,
why can't I have a word, a war,
a whisk for fake thaws midwinter?

                /   /   /

Two boys, seven and four,
I say, a wife. Hazel eyes
(green in light) that tell whichever

truth needs air. These hollow days
I stare into my boys' wide
irises as if they're the stars' ways

to us. At night she comes home coiled
rope. She builds a rock palace
I find while the boys sleep inside.

Then there's one golden hour to practice
a tender much, a slender sloping
touch we forgot, a joint office.

I dream of Father-Knows-Nothing,
my gutted and slumped patron saint
of dads who purport to be writing.

/ / /

Word winter, I have the mid-name taint:
mid-end, mid-field, mid-father, mid-
nothing. This off-kilter complaint.

/ / /

Some days the radio butts in—*lurid*
photo, stab wound, rifle, bomb blast.
One victim tried to speak through liquid—

I turn it off as I defrost a roast
not because the words shouldn't be
here. The world's stray words get lost

inside my sons. They bumblebee
in the left ear, slip onto a road
that snakes past rivers, hide and scurry,

then two nights later the four-year-old
wakes screaming *Spiders with knives!*
Then Saturday, running through a field,

we come upon a deer's cursive
blood tracks. Carcass quartered, gullet
ripped. Our breath grows fricative.

/ / /

Echo chamber of opposites
I want a de-iced word-conduit,
a stay, a brace, a script to forget.

        / / /

Having built myself as opposite
to my father in (I thought) every
way, I see him now opposite

me, in the mirror. I thought poetry
the opposite of business,
set staying home against a history

of leaving. And now I see my chess
is over-simple, my pieces rough-
carved. My fatherly letterpress

is nearly letterless. There's no proof
for making your sons and wife love you—
being there some days isn't enough.

My brother's cancer has moved into
his brain and our talk, occasional,
homesick for never-was, shot-through.

        / / /

In a pine above the snow a cardinal
you fathom on a path a brief freedom
in a song, but something's still atonal.

        / / /

I patch the backyard ice, handle
snow and hot water, know I never
get perfect glass. I have no needle

to patch my brother. I can recover
none of those who fell off the edge
of where we stand: lugubrious, sheer.

I can't hammer in place a bridge
or give my boys bejeweled shelter,
my words to say, my deke, my dodge.

I can't give my love the river,
a trail, a coal-black wood where we
never walk without the other.

On that day that'll come no matter
what, that black mark, that certainty
in a stand of dubious pines, there

after I'm lost for good—finally,
inside these two boys' bodies, I'll be
a tug on their turning, molecular leash.

3

Inside the Wind

Ticking the red haws, lifting dipped
sumac tips, swirling mold inside

leaf piles, swinging the tops of pines
against each other, the wind

reminds me of me: drumming redwood
furrows, scruffing the mutt's thick neck,

ruffling my son's hair. I need
to touch everything to know

it's there. The wind chugs so fast
it pulls off roofs, turns a hawthorn

into a hole, or slows enough
to seem to stop, like it's listening.

I know air rises as it warms
and other cooler air rushes in.

Tell me you never dream
a black box, a hidden engine.

What's inside this inconstant
force, husher and rattler, bender

of grass, flag, tear? If I knew,
I could fix motors: mine, yours.

Mimesis

I say *authenticity, a beating heart,*
then chisel rooms of filigreed cherry
complete with the cheek crease and sinewed effort
of a mouth in mid-surprise. I try to marry
my son's neck tendons taut beneath his scream
with a line that crawls, high-pitched, up the wall,
bellowing, blood-churning, but what I form
can never be close enough to the actual
or far enough from a plowed-over moment
which may not have been what I think. There's space
in this ink box for a rush of color, a point
hooked as it is. My boy there is morose
and poised to never give his dad credit
while here a smile crests, and he gets it.

To My Wife

Nights I pedal a power hammer in the metal shop,
I wake and there is nothing—

not fame, not a long life, not safety—that I want more
than you. But last week

I woke in the night and saw you gripped by some kind
of hand, unconscious:

a body in a deep
current. I know Blake

pounded on catalectic feet; I know how to hit the upper
right corner before the goalie

lifts a glove. Jays weave what was my hair into nests
and my snoring keeps the woodchuck from our peas.

I haven't called the plumber yet and the fridge keeps blinking
its quiet death: 8-8,

8-8. We know how not to fight and how to run a year-
long camp for two good boys

who keep breaking windows in a garage that may never
not be falling down.

Fall is here. A new
gray strand. The new

creases, etched leaf-lines, around your eyes make you more
and more. Rain's needles

melt on the roof, and when I vanish for days into whichever
dark shop I do, that's me hoping I have yet to lose you.

Cracked

I say *poems are good*
and still chew this quiet
until it tells me something
fingers over walkways
buttons eyebrows giving itself
drenched and tired of water
that it wants for skin
bellies—we are so often
deep our cell cities our
more more practice playdates
yet there are still nights
how well our bodies move
transforms our fatigue into
tell and laugh and cry

for nothing or just this one
morning so rare opening
beyond rain thrilling
and roofs and grass tracing
so freely we're all
even when we know and need
petals taproots seedpods
tired these days marrow
stacked papers saying
ten books on dinosaurs
later we remember
together and touch
a story we tell
out and sigh over

The Varieties of Moss on Deer Isle

Twenty-seven years is a blip
for the granite and mica boulders
here, Dad, and all the varieties
of moss that live and die each year
must hold some collective memory
I don't understand in roots and dirt.

I've left the pounding light that blew
our family to pieces—a force
sped into clay, seeking the quickest
path to rest, which was decades.
But I can't name this acrocarp—
it's not *staghorn* or *slender starburst*.

That which made me is in me. Tiny
fragile towers of what might be
boulder broom next to what could be
shy bristle. On the phone my answers
don't fit your one book's descriptions
but I hear you listen. One leaf dropped

can grow a carpet of black earth
hooked to a slab of pink granite.
I'll come to see you. This place
is ancient, enfolds how sorry we hope
to be. My field guide's out of date.
We don't have to name each other.

Mother

No matter hair, no matter
eyebrows, you are now still

the woman who taught me how
to smile. I remember the day

you came home early from work
with a box, the contents of your desk,

because you weren't the one
sleeping with the boss, and you,

single mom with three kids,
rent late, refrigerator empty,

you let the box down
and showed your beautiful teeth.

Making Nothing: Ars Poetica

A poet who once was young and needed a start—
this before his name became a name's name—
who was out of fashion, despairing, yet still
delighted by two crocus blooms gone purple
and closed against a bone-deep wind—like me
he looked to worn-hard things: ax, handle, face;
unrhymed things that see little but wood
to stack, a trinity of muscle, *should,*
and desire for order amid a blown waste
of branches scattered over fields; a sea
of stumps, sticks, and limbs hiding a marble
palace—said, *Paper and time form a mill-*
stone turned by the opposite of fame
and tell you all there is to know of art.

Making Nothing: Arse Poetical

At the Society for This or That's awards,
a minor lord in suit of regulation jeans
and corduroy unfurls his honors

and, sweet Jesus, it takes a while.
I show my teeth because I hate
to be a dick, but so many of the greats

were good at it and, even, I remember,
the not-so-greats, like Robert Bridges,
who no one remembers but when we do

it's as the friend of mud-bottom
and mountain cloudtop, inscape
almost escaped to ether, letter writer:

you are my public.
After Hopkins died, Robert
burned his reply, took decades
to let eyes on his friend's poems.

He could never get over the wind-word
tunnels, funnels of sound, *faults of taste.*
Maybe—once Lord Poem finishes prattling
about greatness and ambiguous homophones—

high-watt verses survive on hip-hop tongues.
We hear in the end when lines move
the hammer, anvil, and stirrup, our hearing bones.

Words with Friends

So many calls I don't have time to make:
to my brother, in conversation with cancer,
my father with his one road washed out—
guns and gold and preserves cocked and ready—
an old friend watching his parents die, and another
who can relive with me all those thousand
hours we spent in chain-link fields with mitts.

Tonight, instead of using my voice to place
a hand on shoulders, I move letters around
a screen for fun, for points, though I hate
that *Qi* on a triple is a better play
than *newborn* or *sister* and even *brother*
is always better than *father* or *mother*. Each word
flies through air to a person who might be

lounging in a flat down the block, in London,
or in an alley shack in Shanghai where
she's pulling up my bank account right now,
draining me of everything while playing
seaside, scoring an extra fifty points,
and sending me a smiley face emoticon
exclamation point. And even as it saves

the game, *quey* will never be a word
that saves me, but *bird, fist, yes, stone, song*
have brought me back. Eyes are the only screens
that matter, and the words we share had better
be better than *joint* or *hex* on a double. I want
a game for words that land in the gut, that shiver
ribs, twitch lips, pop plugged ears, and all
I have is eleven points for this all-time
death-defying rule-filled spit-shine word contest.

Nothing

Not any (material or immaterial) thing.
—Oxford English Dictionary

Not a lawsuit, legal pencil, apple, rainstorm,
not a thing not specified by name, large
or small, not cloud, not sandwich, not penis;

not Oakdale and Pitt, burger flipper, black hole,
runaway truck ramp, fat chewing, lightbulb.

Not lady parts, glitter glue, household gods,
not two bodies sparking like flint and metal,
not *you are mine* or gathering under a name;

neither a place where we kneel and believe,
nor hand-holding, nor Pythagoras, nor time
expanding and contracting like a galaxy;

not a story told while smiling, not personal
effects: notebooks, a ring, a creature, a heart.

Hock, *n.*

Hock doesn't sound
like little purple flowers,
cheap wine, or the last card in the box

but I did know
a pawn shop near Wells
and Elm filled with the saddest gold.

And on the second
Tuesday after Easter
when old parishes once collected

dues and rent
with ale and balloons, some men
would always stand behind the party

with hooked sticks.
I understand: as soon
as we learned to fell a beast

by cutting leg
tendons, we knew it could
be done to a human, meaning we

evolve toward
more efficient ways to hurt
and lose what's buried in a name.

I say *hockey*
and forget the old flowered
injury of the word, my game.

Men's League

Last night's score sheet: snapped stick,
missing helmet screw, a pinkie

I'll never straighten. On the bench
this morning, I lectured two kids

on the best way to get back at
the boy who slashes and trips: *Take*

the puck and score a goal, I said,
like it's the easiest thing. Last night

I did the easiest thing: hit back,
cursed the ref, lowered my head,

and rammed ribs, shoulders. The pinkie
aches, a mark to remember how

badly we want this game to last
past the buzzer and final tally.

Early October

Already the zombie is gleeful
in his feasting on the porch
down the street, a severed
skull lolls, and several
outsized spiders wait
in air above the steps
with sabertooth pincers,

and in a full four weeks
we'll walk, hallowed orange
heads in our hands, soon
filled with Mounds and Snickers
and Almond Joy, my one son
a bloody Coca-Cola,
my other an outlaw with pistol.

And I'm the dad who turns
off the third school shooting
this month—*police found
five guns on him, still
to be fired*—so that the villain
and the can, seven and ten,
won't know this is their world

though they hear they know
exactly how it is poured
across whichever stage
we walk—blood-soaked porch,
blood-soaked streets and grass—
sure as they know I'll smile
and don a mask with dark fangs.

Self-Portrait, with Dish-Rag

Some nights I slip on my brown leather boots
after dinner and announce to the table
I'm headed to a reading. I need magic
thumping in my chest, those tintinnabulations
in my inner ear. The table's probably sticky
because no one cleans up their cantaloupe,

and I hate finding the half-chewed cantaloupe
after I've gone to hear those tintinnabulations
and come back later to that hand-me-down table
of wilting rinds and pools that drip on boots
that Emmett calls *writer boots* for their magic
that makes me taller even when they're sticky.

Fingerprints on white trim, wood floor sticky
with dried juice, and pretzels crushed by boots
that didn't see them set off tintinnabulations
in my head. I want to control it all and can't.
I want unbroken windows, clear floors and table.
I want the house to sweep itself like magic.

I know a house can't clean itself by magic.
The boys and wife all covet cantaloupe
and all admire me in my writer boots,
but everyone's too busy for a sticky
floor someone had better tintinnabulate
the hell out of, along with the table.

It might as well be me: a smooth table,
dining chairs not soiled, walls not sticky
are all a way to tell the cantaloupe's
drooping smiles that this family has magic,

and, look at me, under control, in boots,
making the house sparkle like tintinnabulations

while the others sleep through tintinnabulations
downstairs and dream of kid and doctor magic,
which will make all the surfaces sticky
again. Nothing is more than this table,
where we four sit together with cantaloupe
and talk at night; we don't need the boots.

I know boots are not what hold the magic,
and my sticky life, above and below this table,
tintinnabulates with sweet sweet cantaloupe.

The Last Game

The night my brother's hockey career ended
he'd dangled two and dazzled across the ice
furious scripts the other team couldn't read

when someone's will—maybe a coach's—was done.
A nod, two words: *number nine*. This was '80s
high school hockey, better-tape-your-fingers

hockey, call-the-cops-when-the-stands-empty
hockey, so one kid knelt behind my brother
and another cross-checked him over that knee.

Whoever said the games we play don't have
real stakes? Lee crumpled headfirst into the boards
and lay there until a stretcher carried him.

The doctor said *a few millimeters*
in either direction would have snapped his neck.
And now these doctors measure his game time

in months, not years, not decades. My brother plays
with cranial staples, infusions, endless forms
and learns the rules, penalties, and odds of loss.

After that game, he left the team. I followed
and stuck to empty Sundays, blasting Springsteen
and slap shots on an unguarded net. This game

we'd spent our childhood on, lines and circles,
was gone. Our mom and dad about to split—
our rooms filled with blue lines we never crossed.

Justice in Chicago, 1992

So Duffy rode the El in a sundress
and Sean drove the toll road in a skirt.
I stole my sister's striped mini and heard
wolf whistles near the pawn shop on Wells.

We sashayed in sister's blouses, flounced
in thrift store leggings, laughed—*harmless,*
clever, we thought, talking in lisps, waving
limp wrists, pushing out teenage chests.

After school we crowded into JUG—no mere
detention here, the letters meant *Justice*
Under God—and saw Father's face. Previous
year's seniors lathered oil on wooden stairs

or stole the Dean's stuffed fish and got
a wagged finger, a smirk, a few sharp words.
We'd all agreed to dress in drag. Fifty
or so boys at this school built on boys.

The small JUG room, wood-paneled, promised
that any misstep, shirttail untucked, any
hair over a collar, any skipped class
would be punished. And God's minions—

the fathers we knew not to be alone with,
fathers who coached basketball with a limp,
fathers who juked and swung for gold gloves—
wore not only black and white but plaid

and khaki. I knew how to fold my hands
and keep eyes from the nailed palms and feet
on the wall and from the other crucifixions
heard in crumbling projects across the street.

I knew Mom couldn't afford tuition, knew
she thought I needed a father, and I did,
some pattern to follow, some rooms to hold
all the words I didn't yet know. We looked

at Father's trembling lips and saw we might
as well have pissed in the chapel. He threatened
to hold us out of graduation. Spit
landed on the desk I slouched in up front.

Was it our lisping? Was it the locked box
he'd made to keep himself? And what, what did
we know of those who cross-dressed for real,
crossed lines, crossed the goddamn street?

Turn Strange

A single fork tine's particular curve,
dent in the old metal fire grate,
bicycle tube, limp on a nail,
or little ramp at the end of her nose:

Look long enough for the electrons'
course change, for cattails to be flags
of a marsh nation you enter if
you stop and take in its dank musk.

Look long enough for your son's eyes
to green then become a black
planet with a brown ring inside
a hue you never name. Look

long enough for a blade's letter
on thick pond ice to melt at your touch,
lost path to bliss. Look long enough
for your brother to know whenever,

if ever, he goes, you go, any
distance, any stretch of road
or trip across a dark river
he carries you, you carry him.

Look long enough for sight to become
work, then keep that shovel as piston,
as a load-bearing arm until liquid
salt breaks over you like laughter's
pure verb of lungs and blood and rhythm
not one of us can explain but damn

it's easy. We can look long enough
for the infinitesimal tremors
in our small cell walls to beatbox
together a one two one two.

Listen while I talk on

against time.

—William Carlos Williams

Fields, Roadsides, Throughout

for James Foley, 1973–2014

1

The dog rolls and rolls
(flattened mouse)
spreading a forest
of muck and drizzle
along his fur, and wind
rattles green hands
I mean leaves.
Nothing new
here. I turned off
the news to run
a twisting path
to nowhere to screw
my head on straight.
The news of the woods
blooms:
a redtail circles
a sea of marsh rushes;
a colony of red-
winged blackbirds
(scared by me)
lifts from baskets
of sedge and moss
and skims the cattails;
an egret dips
and arcs, buffeted
by high gusts.
Begin again.
I who so often
shut my mouth

too early
mean to keep on
talking, spurred
until I get to
a sudden meadow,
a king-sized
wish in miniature.

Stinging nettle along the path: well-stalked, coarsely toothed, heart-shaped leaves, the field guide says, and also that there are sixty-one different remedies made with nettles. It flourishes in ruined places. To keep talking means to include some notes too, to let this be messy, to try to get somewhere. Am I a ruined place moving through a ruined place? How to unruin a place? No more nettles then? Where do I find what's multiangled, hollow, and medicinal, what stings?

2

The sky was even larger
and I did nothing
to deserve green hills,
pathside dandelions,
little fields
of trefoil, sweet
clover. And later
still-green raspberries,
nightshade, and lupines.
This day I had time
and actually
saw them (mostly)
and thanked an unseen
unblinking universe
jogging up hills.
I mean I was
jogging—either
around the edge
of the next purple
bend or all
the way up
to Starbird Avenue.

Certain scents and sounds—a squirrel's clicking triggers and dirt musk—sprint the mutts into underbrush, while others—blood from a fox muzzle—lay ears back, put them single file behind me. And what slumps my shoulders for home or widens my pupils to let more wildflower light in?

3

Tonight I go upstairs
last as always
dishes washed
and stacked, doors
and windows checked
to find two boys
huddled together
one side of the bed.
Which do we choose
to remember: older
reading to younger
on a brown couch
or each clawing
the other's eyes,
wanting them out?
I'm tired of poems
puffed, spit shined,
and ultimately
unable to tell
us how to be.
I'd rather the salt-
water cure:
sweat, tears, sea.

*So many cures are temporary, too easy. The little men in my home
want to know all the stories, every one, but there are so many I can't
tell them yet. I try a mild, positive one about the time I saved a man
from drowning in Lake Michigan—a storm, big waves, a little dog in
the swells, the man goes in, then me—then they require extra arms for
holding the smallest hours. They know my brother is sick, the dreaded
C, not the details. But they see my eyes. There are stories outside your
skull, and others within, I want to tell them, as if there's ever a barrier.*

4

The tower of laundry
will not scale itself,
neither the back door
clacking in the wind
shut itself, nor
a trail of mud
pawed from the kitchen
wash itself.
I have no time
for x-ed out words
on median cardboard,
Convict
Addict
nor virtual eyes
as numerous as the stars
one drives sixty miles
to see, not to
mention collapsing
skyscraper icebergs,
whale-bleeding sonar,
brick dust left
by extra large
remote control toys
roaming actual skies,
or lost handwritten
tomes, monkeys
attacking humans
at the water truck,
a K2 of shrink-wrap,
the engineering of meat,
tidal waves
of rhetoric, rivers
dyed blue,

rivers of ones
and zeroes a current
we can't grasp.

No time *is what I say when there are things I don't want to hold. My brother, ninety-eight metastases in his brain, goes in for gamma rays, which sounds like science fiction. Invisible knives guided by a 3-D system to target positions of interest. He goes and goes and goes.*

5

If I wake Emmett
at the wrong hour
his hands shake
eyes open but
not seeing
me, his father,
scared almost out
of his skin,
which means now
I'm awake seeing
my brother who
wants not to be
eaten, his own
skin doing him
in, outside in.
The poppies again,
the small red
palaces of paintbrush
along a path,
cypress, eucalyptus,
and night jasmine
all tell eyes
to be eyes and tell
a nose it still exists.

Tell me what exists of James Foley, a teacher, writer, and journalist I almost knew—out together once in Manhattan with a common friend. He looked in my eye. He taught and wrote and chased stories knowing exactly how dank, how sharp these were—forty-four days etched into his skin before they released him from Libya.

He went back. To know any danger that well and do the task and do the task still still because you know no one else will. He needed to tell us how bad it might be. He was taken and held, seconds dripping into years. He never came back from Syria. He became a video clip I cannot not see, another reason to run in the woods, another reason to be quiet at home. By the law of conservation of mass, he's now in the sunflowers, asters, jasmines, and roadside weeds.

6

I'm still here,
yes, still talking,
stretching the breeze
until it's so thin
it lasts forever.
A doctor taught me
how to talk like this
and I never listened
until I needed a way
to stop the day in mid-
tick, so I could
bury my head
into its skin, suck
as much blood
as I could hold.
Once I've had enough,
fat with detail
I'll drop off
into the tall grasses
and wait, let
the hours go,
let myself sink
into dirt.

How many hours spent fiddling with words this week instead of earning an honest wage? How many ribs trembled by stories I threw dirt on? Easier to disappear, to sink into dirt. If I divide Lee's tumors by Jim's particles whipping around the earth on a desert wind, what's left to tell my sons?

7

No, no, not
the tick, that easy
exit. It crawled
a leg—I pinched
then flushed it.
This will go on
at least until
I see why I run
the same path over
and over, fold
the same shirts
back and again,
grieve the bodies
the same: barely
moving a muscle.
My body
is a tuning fork
and someone keeps
hitting high C.
I don't choose what
I see—I don't
mean look at
I mean see:
wind in tall grass
sculpting temporary
hands and texts
or rubble that moans
and claws its own
eyes. It's all seen
the sheen off mud
or blood but that
seed is buried
until I run

a path and thrumming
inside matches
a hooked bloom
vermillion burst
from *another common*
flower that grows
in waste places.

5

Self-Help

Resist the urge to start the day
with what other people think.
Dig for that cerulean sky
in your blood last night, rock pink
bloom, or prayer for a brother
about to become a scalpel.
What click or digital trash will bother
its way into your latest gospel?
Or what bark, what animated flips
(hairpin midair) might unsay
what your kid said? Forget your lips
to find an empty roadway where
your coronary artery used to be
and hear that crooked, quiet sea.

Bottom Line

Forty-three years in on a death
sentence. Clauses arrange
a dissociation of syntax.

Henry, a few headaches in,
wakes and can't read, a tumor
crowding his brain. My mom

doesn't feel well after dinner
and they find it wrapped around
her ovaries. One dog chews

its bed; the other breathes
heavy against the wood floor.
On the phone with my father

when I talk, I slant and slant.
Do I need a permission slip?
my youngest asks. I chew my bed

and sleep short, fretful hours,
then wake with iron and hammer
six words onto one true line.

Low

I tug at the weights on the pulleys inside my cheeks and make them
     move
so I can smile for my sons, mutts, and love.

Whether or not I admit to standing lost in a valley of pine,
a faulty mechanism beats overtime:

my brother stands, riddled, brimmed, two thousand miles away—
with nodules doctors try to solve. They deploy

tiny cameras and armies and know the stakes: wife, kids, life.
Here, piles of socks and underwear vouchsafe

solutions. Same with crusted stacks of plates and bowls in the sink,
homework with Xs, and orange crates, and a bank.

What of the other twenty-two hours? A friend dealt with that truth
by cocking the shadow in his mouth.

Some rain right now would be indulgent but also true: squall
is to porch as circulating tumor cell

is to smile. One son needs eggs; his brother—the younger, like me—
to be read to. My voice rattles: *Coming.*

Going to Church

Church of the smallest word,
church of the eyeball and robins tuning morning light,
church of dog tongue,
                    of sidewalk riven by daisies,
                    of a high and tight fastball,
                    of the shape and smell
                    of my beloved's side of the bed,
church of bricks that yesterday were building,
        of bread and butter and a bottle of beer,
        of creekstone and silver elm,
        of voices we hear, asking in the still
        dark for a body to give them breath,
church of a quaver carried thousands of miles
        and given to the tiny bones inside an ear,
screenless, windowless church
        of a twisting northern wind,
        of the night when a wall of trees too thick
            to see through called to my car,
        of visions I shook from eyes
            and claimed I didn't see,
I kneel here. I bring
a tin cup of water to my lips.

Making Nothing: Why I Write Poems

Genesis monsoon:
sheets and torrents

roofs cracking open
their tiniest holes

to rivulets and
ropes, creeks

bubbling sidewalks,
white water pulsing

across streets
down the avenue.

The dogs scratch
until I acquiesce.

A way to pour
a self out, to happen

through hedge, through forest
end without end.

My chin drips,
pools in sneakers,

and I find two
odd specimens:

one down near the deep edge
of the king tide I fear,

the other between
two railroad ties—

stones I pocket,
carry back, and add

to the leaning tower
of things I will

never explain
so I keep them close.

Deked, Again

Sometimes you dangle
        the puck, pull it
back, and a tank-
        shouldered giant
with a hooked stick
        pins his eyes
like a boutonniere
        on a prom lapel
and plants his gloves
        in your sternum.

After the doctor
        scans—poisons
and scans—and one
        of many tumors
in your brain doesn't
        shrink like the others
but grows stubborn
        as a crocus in snow,
he cuts open
        your frontal lobe.

I write your eulogy
        in my head, see
myself in front
        of a crowd, see
the obituary's flat
        font in the paper,
put my left hand
        on your youngest's arm.
I count you gone.
        I'm not proud.

And you, more than
       a lesson I learned
about breathing
       next to a droplet
on a leaf, more than
       a decoy for me,
are my blood most
       like unlike me
and still you teach
       as you once taught—

Try to get past me—
       that each morning
a defenseman stands
       with his stick waiting
to see how you
       will try to entice him—
force, will, quickness,
       simple pleas—
back into his cage.
       A six-year-long

game, and counting.
       The defenseman waits
whether we
       see him or not
and each day now
       I watch how you
keep your head
       on a swivel, wait
for the pass, then
       find an extra gear.

The Latest in Nanotechnology

This *small, handheld device*
perhaps crafted by microbes
or robots the size of dust mites

who crawl with hammers thinner
than hairs and lyres made of air
into the ears of anyone

who reads this, like you,
in order to make a delicious,
somber, jubilant, nighttime

trash-can, pebble-thrown opera
that unfolds across a screen
the size of your eyes, the size

of a sky just turned to blue dark
& now rising in windows
the dark shapes of trees,

so all the little birds tune
their giant songs & you too
contain a song bigger

than your body—well, no
and yes, this is the newest
technology, meaning

ancient, an app with a code
from the time of magic, which is
a word we used when we

couldn't understand how
a thing leapt from a page
like this one into your ears

into your throat—the words
so old they're new and known
and felt, green between finger-

tips, heat in the heart,
and no, this paper will not
sync with seawater, it is not

compatible with certain
chemicals or every tongue,
it will not reforest vast tracts,

it does not matter to any-
one who doesn't enter
this small and giant door,

an entryway created
to give permission to see
this ball of fire above

the small, mistaken, human
endeavors now cranking:
begin again.

Hockey Dad

Once you have ice blocks for feet, icicle fingers,
and a lump in your throat to tremble your body
with cold tomorrow, you doubt the sanity

of waking at five, the eight-year-old on ice
by six, blades carving shapes you can't name.
And when your boy looks through his coach's face

on the bench, with red cheeks, a fire in each wooded
eye, and complains about tripping—that number
sixteen with the black mask—says *I'll chop*

him down next time, you doubt this game.
At the hour you venture into the warm room
to thaw out your spine and hear a father

break down his son's backhand highlight spinner
in a voice loud enough for all to hear,
you know the annual backyard ice sheet

was a bad idea. But also remember
all those hours with your friends and brother—
legs pushed until muscles wailed, then sang—

knocked down, scrambling up again, skating
the last tenths off the clock, down, up, bearing
each sore ounce, each breath and every

sinew, humbling yourself to the rules of a game
and the flawed eyes of a referee—and then ask,
Is this such bad training for what is to come?

Making Nothing: The Volume Up to Eleven

Nights when it's not at all hard to boil me, my boys
say *suck* and *stupid* and *words don't matter, Dad,*

and all who've struggled to spit their tang and slush and tic
and all who've cooked them down to burnt pans smoking
and all who've fought tooth and bone with batons or with
a furious self both handed down and made by hand

flash in me, and I—part all, part self—flash, my gut
in charge of throat and mouth and lips, and we slam doors
in the way I was taught. Which are the words that don't matter:
the ones spoken during the fight or the ones after?

Clever's never enough—a poem is part fist
part petal-born and riding, delighting, unhidden from dying.

My Brother Dying

For almost seven years now
my brother daily makes
a gruel of kefir, oil, and flax,

and eats it with a spoon.
When a doctor says you won't
see your kids' next birthdays

and you live six more
with them, you eat gruel.

Then a new spot on your liver
appears on a scan, growing
a collection of mistakes—

replicating and replicating.
Two weeks of thinking:

Last stack of plates in the sink.
Last run on a mountain path,
your dog testing the wind.

Last time you open a door
for your wife or tuck sheets tight
for one son, loose for the other.

Then a doctor says, *We think
the spot's a blip,* and you're back
to dying like us, and daily gruel.

Dive

A new tumor
on his heart
doesn't sound
like the ones
on other organs—
On his heart?
And now what
treatment? Watch
the clock? Follow
a salt road out
as far as its end?
Remember he's still
here? Send clips?
A center's sick
dangle—showing
what he makes
disappear—or a wing
who blurs by, blades
and limbs, then spins
360 degrees
outside time
spinorama?
Send a heart
emoji?
      In hockey
a dive is when
a player acts
hurt and falls
so that the ref
calls a penalty.
Here it's something
else. A brother

dazzles (annoys,
enrages, awes,
leads) his younger
for forty-four
years. Then
the elder begins
a fall. Or maybe
this descent only
acted like
other motion
all along. Maybe
all our motion
is down. Where
is the ref? What
happens next in
this moment, then
another, a center
my brother skates
off to find?

NOTES

"High Forest State Marginal" takes its title from four streets in Portland, Maine.

"The Varieties of Moss on Deer Isle" is after Robert Hass.

"Nothing" was granted existence by the Oxford English Dictionary's definition of the word.

Among the sources of "Hock, *n.*" is Hockenday, an annual festival described in the poem. From the Hocktide Court Book, Hungerford, 1583: "Ffirst for the mayntenance and better contynuance of the ancient franchises of the same Towne, there ys and tyme out of mynde always hath bene kept and holden on the Tuysday called Hockenday evry yere one Courte called Hocktide Courte in the Comon Hall there at the howre of eight of the Clock in the fforenone of the same day."

"Self-Portrait, with Dish-Rag" borrows its end words from a sestina by Emily Hollyday.

"Turn Strange" is after an exhibit of works by Duncan Hewitt called "Turning Strange" at the Portland Museum of Art.

"Fields, Roadsides, Throughout" owes a debt to William Carlos Williams.

"The Latest in Nanotechnology" is for Wesley McNair. The italicized phrase is taken from one of his poems.

ACKNOWLEDGMENTS

Many thanks to the editors of the journals and magazines where many of these poems first appeared, often in different form:

Broadsided: "Hockey Poem"
The Café Review: "At Sea," "Making Nothing: So Much Depends"
Connotation Press: *An Online Artifact*: "Cracked"
december: "Going to Church"
FIELD: "High Forest State Marginal," "To My Wife"
jubilat: "Ars Poetica," "Mock Heroic"
The Literary Review: "Hockey Dad," "Men's League"
The Maine Review: "Unwritten"
Poetry Northwest: "Inside the Wind"
Prairie Schooner: "The Varieties of Moss on Deer Isle"
Slice: "Self-Help," "Wing and a Prayer"
UMVA Quarterly: "Turn Strange"
the Under Review: "Deked, Again"

"Self Portrait, with Dish-Rag" appears in *The Story I Want to Tell: Explorations in the Art of Writing* (Tilbury House, 2014).

"Mock Heroic" also appeared on Verse Daily on January 24, 2015.

"Early October" and "Words with Friends" appeared on Maine Public Radio's *Poems from Here* in 2018.

"Going to Church" was chosen as a finalist for *december*'s 2020 Jeff Marks Memorial Poetry Prize by Aimee Nezhukumatathil.

These poems took a long time to gestate, and many people helped along the way. In particular, there was a weekend on Mount Desert Island when Christian Barter, Matt O'Donnell, and Jeffrey Thomson told me this was a book and helped me envision it. Thanks also to Linda Aldrich, Colin Cheney, Marita O'Neil, Dawn Potter, Betsy Sholl, and Kathleen Sullivan for their clear eyes and full hearts on a number of these poems and to Craig Teicher for his ear and insights. Thanks to Lewis Robinson and too many hockey buddies to name who asked after these poems and this book and helped me keep the faith.

My brother, Leland Fay, read an earlier draft of this book before he died and gave it his blessing, which I am deeply grateful for since many of these poems reference his experience. To say that his example has shaped and will continue to shape my life is a tremendous understatement.

Nothing I write is possible without my family, and all of it, always, is for them: Liam, Emmett, and Renée.

CAVANKERRY'S MISSION

A not-for-profit literary press serving art and community, CavanKerry is committed to expanding the reach of poetry and other fine literature to a general readership by publishing works that explore the emotional and psychological landscapes of everyday life, and to bringing that art to the underserved where they live, work, and receive services.

OTHER BOOKS IN THE
EMERGING VOICES SERIES

Deke Dangle Dive has been set in Acumin Pro, a neo-grotesque sans-serif typeface intended for a balanced and rational quality. It was designed by Robert Slimbach for Adobe in 2015.